This journal belongs to

_____

GARY THOMAS

A LIFELONG LOVE

Devotional Journal

BELLE
★ CITY ★
GIFTS

Belle City Gifts™
Racine, WI 53403

Belle City Gifts is an imprint of the BroadStreet Publishing Group, LLC
www.broadstreetpublishing.com

A LIFELONG LOVE
Devotional Journal

By Gary Thomas with Nathanael White

Inspired by *A Lifelong Love: What If Marriage Is about More Than Just Staying Together?*
By Gary Thomas (Oct. 1, 2014, David C. Cook)

ISBN-13: 9781424549689

Cover and interior design by Garborg Design Works, Inc. | www.garborgdesign.com

Printed in China

Many waters

cannot quench love;

rivers cannot

sweep it away.

SONG OF SONGS 8:7

Booker T. Washington was born a slave, yet became a surprising political force in the nineteenth century. He believed that when difficulties call out your best, they become stepping-stones instead of roadblocks.

Maybe you feel your marriage is filled with more difficulties than blessings. Perhaps you feel you have nothing to give, that your relationship is stuck in a rut, or that you and your spouse lack what it takes to achieve the happiness you desire.

If that's you, I have good news: Marriage is not about what we have, but about what we do with what we have.

There is always hope. Your marriage, yes yours, can become an inspiration to other couples. Your marriage can become fruitful and fulfilling. Your marriage can become a source of profound joy, rich togetherness, and powerful witness.

I wrote this journal as a tool to help guide you through the process of taking what you have—difficulties or blessings—

and turning them into stepping-stones for a lifelong love and a beautiful marriage. The theme for each day is carefully designed with this purpose in mind, beginning with thought-provoking content followed by a powerful question to provide direction as you journal.

This journaling is where you will find transformation. Be honest with yourself. Open your heart freely to God in this process. Allow Him to speak to you and help you. Then begin to apply the simple principles you find on each page.

Step by step, day by day, moment by moment, you will find life and joy growing in your marriage. More than that, you will find greater fulfillment in giving your marriage—and your whole life—to God.

Then, beginning with God lavishing His love on you, your marriage will grow…

…into A Lifelong Love.

Build the Right Foundation

Marriage is designed by God, a mark of His kindness because He allows us to know the joys of intimacy and family life. Yet even the best of marriages is a miserable substitute for the ultimate reality of living for God. Unless…

Unless we have a magnificent obsession, an overriding purpose that ties our days together, gives comfort in the valleys, calls us forward in the suffering, highlights our joy, and even seasons our ecstasies.

That's what God provides in a marriage based on Him.

"If you remain in me and I in you, you will bear much fruit; apart from me you can do nothing." —John 15:5

What do you think it looks like to have God as your magnificent obsession?

Living for God

Nothing, not even marriage, can substitute for kingdom life, because that's how God created us. It might be possible to offer five steps to help your marriage be a little less miserable, but nothing can substitute for keeping God's kingdom first.

Marriage is a lot of wonderful things, but it is not our reason for being. To expect it to become that is to smother it. But when we allow God to be our reason for being and place Him first, it frees our marriages to be filled with the good God desires for them.

"Seek first his kingdom and his righteousness, and all these things will be given to you as well." —Matthew 6:33

Write a letter telling God what you desire for your marriage. How does living for Him affect those desires?

Starting with God's Love

Perhaps you feel you bring a lot to your marriage. Perhaps you feel you bring very little. Either way, when God becomes part of the equation, what we bring doesn't matter anymore. What matters is what He brings.

Three elements—drawing near to God, pursuing real love, and intentionally pursuing each other—build a stable base upon which good marriages grow. They place our hope in God and not in ourselves.

A good marriage isn't about us; it's about God and what He brings. Place God at the center of your marriage today.

"I have loved you with an everlasting love; I have drawn you with unfailing kindness." —JEREMIAH 31:3

What does it mean to you that God loves you with an everlasting love?

God Is Your Father-In-Law

If your spouse is saved, then God sees them as His child. That makes Him not just your Father, but also your Father-in-Law.

Consider that, and then think about this: How would you feel if a daughter-in-law treated your son the way you treat your husband? Or how would you feel if a son-in-law treated your daughter the way you treat your wife?

I want to be a faithful son-in-law, one who makes God sigh with satisfaction when He watches how I care for and treat my wife, His daughter.

See what great love the Father has lavished on us, that we should be called children of God! —1 John 3:1

Write a letter to your present or future son- or daughter-in-law about how you want them to treat your child. Then read the letter to yourself as though God wrote it to you about your spouse.

Connect Marriage
with Worship

I used to think I needed to pray for a better marriage until one day God convicted me (through 1 Peter 3:7) that I needed a better marriage so that I can pray.

Look at God through the lens of Father-in-Law to understand this. If a young man came to me, praising me, even giving me ten percent of his income, and all the while I knew he was abusing or neglecting one of my daughters, I'd have nothing to say to him except, "Hey, start treating my daughter better, and then we can talk."

The integrity of your worship of God depends on you treating your spouse well.

"First go and be reconciled to them; then come and offer your gift."
—MATTHEW 5:24

How does it change the way you see your spouse when you remember he or she is God's child?

Stop Prosecuting, Start Defending

If we truly want to love God's sons and daughters, we have to seek to understand them. Have you ever asked God why your spouse is the way he or she is?

It's true our spouses make mistakes that hurt us. However, we can have empathy for others even while despising what they are doing.

We must be for our spouses as God is for us. Do you realize that in the height of your rebellion against God, He was for you? That's how God treated you. God simply asks that we give the same grace we have received.

God demonstrates his own love for us in this: While we were still sinners, Christ died for us. —ROMANS 5:8

Ask God to show you how He sees your spouse. Write what you feel He says to you about your spouse.

Keep Perspective

Many marriage books promise a new spouse by the weekend, and oh, I wish that were always true. But what if change takes longer to happen? What if it never happens?

Whether or not changes happen in our marriages, what needs to change is our perspective. Instead of only considering our desires for this life—a fulfilling marriage, rich relationships, an easy life— we must consider how God will reward in heaven our faithful stewardship on earth.

If we are living for life in the new heavens and the new earth, the spiritual riches that await us will help us maintain proper spiritual priorities in the here and now.

God "will repay each person according to what they have done."
—Romans 2:6

Imagine yourself standing before God. What do you want to hear Him say about your faithfulness in your marriage?

Don't Settle Before the Destination

When I drove from Houston, Texas, to Portland, Oregon, I made progress every day. I didn't get lost in Colorado Springs; I didn't buy a home in Rawlins, Wyoming. I passed right through Ogden, Utah, because I knew there was a destination that I had to reach.

All of us need to view this life as a journey, not as a final destination. Marriage is just one aspect of this journey.

Never forget your magnificent obsession. He is preparing something eternal for you that is far greater than any human marriage could ever be.

I press on toward the goal to win the prize for which God has called me heavenward in Christ Jesus. —Philippians 3:14

Describe a marriage you think is worthy of heavenly reward. Ask God to help you make your marriage like this.

"How Well Did You Love?"

The Lord will reward us for whatever good we do, not whatever good we receive (2 Corinthians 5:10). I will be rewarded, not for how my wife loved me, but for how I loved my wife.

If I am living for today, a good day is when Lisa notices me, appreciates me, and makes my life more enjoyable. Living for eternity means a good day is when I notice Lisa, appreciate Lisa, serve Lisa, and make her life more enjoyable, because that's what will be rewarded at the judgment seat of Christ.

"Love your enemies, do good to them, and lend to them without expecting to get anything back. Then your reward will be great."
—Luke 6:35

What would you say to God if He asked you, "How well did you love?"

Embrace the Hope of Heaven

Maybe you are married to the godliest, kindest, most thoughtful spouse who ever lived. If so, that is your reward. But you can still store up heavenly reward in other ways.

What if you pray for your spouse, support them, and encourage them so they become more than they ever would have been single? You will have literally set them up for multiple blessings in the next life!

Living for heaven is not about checking out of earth. It's about checking into earth with a new intensity as God's redeeming work reveals itself through us and sets us up for eternal rewards.

Let us consider how we may spur one another on toward love and good deeds. —Hebrews 10:24

How is the hope of heaven influencing the way you love your spouse?

Trust the Holy Spirit

Can you imagine how much more Jesus could have done in another thirty years on earth? He could have written so many books, established churches, and left detailed instructions that would have spared the church centuries of debate.

But Jesus didn't do that. That's how much He trusted the Holy Spirit to teach and guide us.

Do you trust the Holy Spirit to help build your marriage? He is a powerful force to help us, lifting us above selfishness and weak love to embrace the glorious strength of God loving through us.

"You will receive power when the Holy Spirit comes on you." —ACTS 1:8

What does it mean to you that God is with you to help you in your marriage?

Power for the Powerless

God will call us to various tasks for which we lack enough power on our own. Marriage is such a task.

The good news is that there is no marriage failing so badly that God can't redeem it. God will never call us to do something without giving us everything that is necessary to finish the task. It may not be all that we think we need, but it will be all that we do need.

The secret, then, to a truly sacred marriage is a person—God's promised Holy Spirit.

He gives strength to the weary and increases the power of the weak.
—Isaiah 40:29

Write a letter to God telling Him about how His power can help your marriage.

Stay Fueled

There isn't a car in existence that can keep going without refueling. And there isn't a marriage that can keep pressing into sacred intimacy without daily drawing on God's presence and power.

Our primary human relationship makes us dependent on our primary divine relationship every day. We can keep trying to draw from an empty well—trying to transform our marriages by asking a stubborn or unfeeling spouse to meet our needs, or we can ask the God who promised to pour out His Spirit on all who seek Him for what we need.

If we truly want to transform our marriages, we must learn the glory of divine dependence.

"I will pour out my Spirit." —Acts 2:18

What are your favorite ways to "refuel" your intimacy with the Holy Spirit?

Hold On to Promise

Your marriage began with a promise, and God has made a promise to you—to give you strength when you are weak.

What is marriage calling you to right now, even today, that you don't feel capable of doing on your own? Instead of saying, "This is just too hard," or, "This just isn't my gifting or calling," why not hold God to His word?

Let's allow the difficulties of marriage to teach us the glory of spiritual dependence on God, tapping into that glorious, fierce force that exists outside ourselves.

"My grace is sufficient for you, for my power is made perfect in weakness." —2 Corinthians 12:9

Write a prayer to God and offer your weaknesses to Him. Ask Him to give you His strength in the midst of them.

Discover a Mission

Why did you get married?

Most people marry because they say they fell in love, but this should only be a first step. If love creates a desire to be married, mutual purpose then fulfills the mission of marriage. A lack of purpose is like a diseased heart that continually slows us down; a shared sense of purpose is like a defibrillation machine giving us another chance.

If our mission from Christ is to "seek first the kingdom of God," how can a successful God-honoring marriage not be marked by mission? When we give away our life, we find it. When we focus outside our marriage, we end up strengthening our marriage.

God blessed them and said to them, "Be fruitful and increase in number; fill the earth and subdue it." —GENESIS 1:28

What mission could you and your spouse begin to pursue together?

Seek God's Kingdom First

Living for God's mission makes life so much simpler. Imagine the impact it would have just in marital conflict if we only prayed how Jesus taught us to pray.

What if our first prayer was, "Father, bring your kingdom rule to my heart, marriage, and this house?" It would change many things, because often the approach is, "God, change him," or, "God, make her appreciate me."

Start with God's kingdom first. Then Jesus promises, "All these things will be added to you." Try it, and you'll see.

"This, then, is how you should pray:
'Our Father in heaven...your kingdom come, your will be done,
on earth as it is in heaven.'" —Matthew 6:9–10

What changes do you see happening as you make Jesus' prayer your first prayer?

Embrace Purposeful Passion

Almost five hundred years ago, William Tyndale was burned at the stake solely for translating Scripture into an accessible language. During the days before his death, Tyndale boldly told a clergyman, "If God spare my life, I will cause the boy that drives the plough to know more of the Scripture than you do."

Though Tyndale's life was cut short, his mission was accomplished. Easily accessible versions of Scripture soon covered the European continent and laid the groundwork for the English Reformation.

It all began with a mission. What is your mission?

Then I heard the voice of the Lord saying, "Whom shall I send? And who will go for us?" And I said, "Here am I. Send me!" —ISAIAH 6:8

Personalize Tyndale's statement for yourself, "If God spare my life, I will…"

Think Like a Monk

We need to be married people with a monk's heart. This might seem a tad difficult, but consider how many marital arguments result from disappointments with our spouses?

We expect them to do or say something they just don't, so we feel hurt. We think, "If they truly loved me, they would know, right?" While we may feel this way sometimes, it is an impossible burden for any spouse to carry.

A "monk's marriage" is solely dependent on God, looking to Him alone to meet our needs. Then, instead of resentment at what your spouse doesn't do, you'll be overwhelmed with gratitude for every little thing he or she does do.

Cast all your anxiety on him because he cares for you. —1 PETER 5:7

How would you feel if your spouse released you from needing to meet his or her needs?

Seek God's Approval

Everyone likes to be noticed and appreciated, but this can quickly become a wrong focus that drains life from our marriages.

When we begin to view these sentiments as rights we can demand from our spouses, it's a sign that our hearts are focused on the wrong person. We need to seek approval from, and faithfulness to, the God before whom we will stand one day.

God will not ask us on that day how encouraged or noticed we were, but how much we encouraged and noticed others.

I press on toward the goal to win the prize for which God has called me heavenward in Christ Jesus. —Philippians 3:14

When you stand before God, what do you want Him to say about how you treated your spouse?

Become Gentle and Humble

Even bigger than any goal we have for our marriages is the calling God has for them.

Our job is to build a marriage worthy of that calling—the advancement of God's kingdom. To have a marriage worthy of our calling, we need to be gentle and humble. This is how Jesus described Himself, and how He promised to treat His bride, the church.

When we become gentle and humble in our marriages, we create a marriage where the character of Jesus is displayed for all to see. That is a marriage worthy of our calling.

I urge you to live a life worthy of the calling you have received. Be completely humble and gentle. —Ephesians 4:1–2

How do you think you and your spouse would respond to being treated more gently and humbly?

Meet Sin with Grace

You aren't married to a perfect person, and you also aren't perfect. This isn't new information. We all falter at times. So how do we respond to failure and sin?

We respond with grace. We are sensitive and encouraging about each other's weaknesses and quirks. We do this with joy and a good spirit, celebrating the unique expression of God's creative genius.

This calls us to a nurturing marriage instead of an attacking marriage. We should have the concern of a physician, wanting them to get well, rather than the passion of a prosecuting attorney, wanting to make them pay.

We all stumble in many ways. —James 3:2

What do you appreciate most about your spouse's unique differences and quirks?

Protect Unity

God has called us to a ministry of reconciliation—God reconciling the world to Himself, and us being reconciled to each other.

This requires us to guard our marriages, feed them, work through issues, confront when necessary if something is threatening our unity, forgive with eagerness to preserve our unity, be gentle so that no bitterness attacks our unity, live with patience so that we don't replay past episodes, and certainly remain vigilant to never let our heart be stolen by anyone else.

We talk things through. We forgive. We don't stonewall. We pursue reconciliation and understanding. This is a life worthy of our calling.

Make every effort to keep the unity of the Spirit through the bond of peace. —Ephesians 4:3

Which of the unity-building actions listed here challenged you the most? How can you begin improving in that area even today?

Revere Christ

The apostle Paul revered Christ Jesus, and that reverence shaped the way he treated people. His unchanging reverence for Christ, who is continually worthy of reverence, formed the foundation for how he treated even sinful people.

If our motivation to love our spouse is always based on reverence for God, nothing can ever shake it. No rationalizing. No searching for a onetime exclusion. If I call myself a Christian, I have certain marital obligations that not even my spouse can discharge me from.

Marriage isn't primarily about us, but about Christ and the church. It is a picture of the gospel before it is a vehicle of happiness. It's a prophetic call before it is a playground of romanticism.

Submit to one another out of reverence for Christ. —EPHESIANS 5:21

Write to God how you feel about this commitment to revere Him first in your marriage.

Do Your Part

Husbands and wives each have their own duties, and our duties are all we have charge over. We can't do our spouse's duties, so why fret over whether or not they are doing their part? We must simply focus on doing our part.

This is what reverence to Christ calls us to—it removes our commitment to and practice of marriage from the changing whims of an imperfect partner and places it on the never-changing foundation of reverence for Christ.

Wives, submit yourselves to your own husbands…Husbands, love your wives, just as Christ loved the church. —EPHESIANS 5:22, 25

Write a letter to your spouse, forgiving them for failing to do their duty for you and recommitting to do your duty to them.

Find True Happiness

Doing our duty doesn't squeeze the romance or enjoyment out of marriage; on the contrary, it preserves it.

Marriages based on a person's behavior are doomed to rise or fall with a spouse's mood. Marriages based on the eternal relationship of Christ and the church will be filled with joy and fulfillment.

Living life in a way that is worthy of the call of Christian marriage is our top priority. Doing our duty is the only thing that will lead to true marital happiness and satisfaction—regardless of what our circumstances or spouses' responses may be.

Be devoted to one another in love. Honor one another above yourselves.
—ROMANS 12:10

How do you feel about this statement: "Doing your duty preserves the romance and enjoyment of your marriage"?

Be Yourself

Don't compare yourself with other couples to measure your happiness; compare your obedience with God's design on your life to measure your faithfulness.

We're just Gary and Lisa. That's all we're called to be. We have no other marriage to live up to, no other couple that should make us feel ashamed, humiliated, envious, or proud. In the same way, God has established your marriage, and that's the life He wants you to live.

Become comfortable with your story—your identity as a couple. Relish it. Never compare it. Just be faithful to the unique vision God has given to the unique you. God wants to release and bless the couple that is you.

"Come, follow me," Jesus said. —MATTHEW 4:19

Without comparing your marriage to other marriages, what do you consider your marriage's strengths? Why?

Find Focus

There are many personality tests that form a scientific way to approach relationships, and they can be helpful.

However, plenty of couples have risen above natural limitations to achieve more relationally than a test says might be possible. We cannot base our marriages on compatibility more than mission.

Purpose can be more concrete than personality because God redeems our characters. Embracing the magnificent obsession can even overcome challenges in compatibility because, in the unity of the Spirit, you can join around a common mission.

Agree with one another in what you say...that there be no divisions among you, but that you be perfectly united in mind and thought.
—1 Corinthians 1:10

What can you and your spouse find together as your joint purpose? Brainstorm ideas.

Conquer

I'm currently working with a couple who may not make it. They went to an intensive marriage rescue weekend, but it didn't take. One of them has an entrenched attitude that nothing will ever change, so why bother?

A defeatist attitude kills almost as many marriages as do affairs. If you are frustrated in any area of your marriage, will you choose to live by your past experience or by the truth of God's Word? Do you view yourself as more than a conqueror or as one of the conquered? With God, the choice is yours.

In all these things we are more than conquerors through him who loved us. —ROMANS 8:37

Tell God about the area of your marriage where you feel the most defeated. Ask Him to help you see yourself as more than a conqueror in that area.

More Than Conquer

It can be easy to get stuck thinking only about the problems in our marriages and forget to think about life after the problem is resolved.

Don't let your vision get trapped in the problem. Keep vision for your marriage beyond the problems you face. Then, step by step, conquer them.

First, conquer yourself. Remember you are in charge of your love. Your spouse can't force you to close your heart to them. Second, conquer your home. Stay immersed in Scripture to make your home a place where God reigns supreme. Third, more than conquer by spreading your victories to a world that needs them.

If God is for us, who can be against us? —ROMANS 8:31

Think of the greatest problem you face in your marriage and answer this: "After we get through this, how do you think God might use us?"

Keep Building

Popular thinking treats marriage like planting a tree seedling. At first, you water it and weed around it, but after a year or two, you can ignore it and the tree just grows.

That's how most couples live. They'll talk about their pasts when they first meet, get engaged, and go through premarital counseling. But after the wedding, the marriage is supposed to somehow "finish itself" just by the fact that it exists.

Every season of life tempts us to stop building our marriages. But a marriage relationship isn't built until the wedding, it's built until "death do us part."

Each one should build with care. —1 Corinthians 3:10

What does it look like to you to build your marriage every day?

Cultivate Real Intimacy

Many marriages are plagued with artificial intimacy. It begins with infatuation, which is notoriously short-lived.

But most couples don't notice when it ends. By the time infatuation wanes, they are caught in the artificial intimacy of planning a wedding, which leads to establishing a house, which leads to raising children.

These couples have to realize they've been living relationally on shared tasks, not shared intimacy. They're teammates, not spouses, and when the season is over, what do teammates do? They go their own ways.

Don't get caught with artificial intimacy. Instead, build the real thing.

Place me like a seal over your heart, like a seal on your arm; for love is as strong as death. —Song of Songs 8:6

Do you feel more connected to your spouse than you did on your wedding day? Why do you think that is?

Make Your Marriage

A good marriage isn't something you find; it's something you have to keep on making. Just as importantly, you can also begin remaking it at any stage.

What's so sad is when couples often say, "I must have married the wrong person," instead of, "We haven't nurtured the relationship."

If you believe a good marriage is something you find and yours isn't working, you can't fix that, and often the only logical solution is divorce. But if you believe a good marriage is something you make and it's not working, you can choose to build it up in a different way.

The wise woman builds her house, but with her own hands the foolish one tears hers down. —Proverbs 14:1

Write three ideas for how you can begin nurturing an area of your marriage that's in need.

Watch Out for Bumps

Life brings changes. Marriage is a change we choose, but marriage leads to other changes. And each change requires communication.

Some bumps include the death of infatuation, the birth of kids, the busyness of raising children, the quiet of the empty nest, a sudden change in midlife, or the medical diagnosis of an aging body. Whatever it is, we can choose to let it be an avenue toward intimacy, or a highway toward gradual separation.

These bumps can be like billboards, shifting our focus off of what's most important. Examine your marriage. Did you lose sight of your spouse when you hit one of these bumps?

Catch for us the foxes, the little foxes that ruin the vineyards.
—Song of Songs 2:15

Have you had a difficult life-change in your marriage? What could you say to your spouse to spark your intimacy afresh?

Reconnect

Marriage is a bit like snorkeling. We can go underwater for a while, but eventually we have to come up for air.

Life dictates that we may not be able to connect as often as we would like. We may have to endure short separations to care for our parents and children. But when the seasons never end—when one season is replaced by another—our marriages will slowly suffocate.

Do you want an increasingly intimate union? Then you must work to stay close. Be eager to get back together when life events force you apart. As a couple, you can hold your breath for only so long.

I belong to my beloved, and his desire is for me.
—Song of Songs 7:10

Choose a few simple (yet significant) things you will do this week to pursue your spouse.

Say, "I Will"

An intimate marriage requires vigilance. Just waking up and going about our days, without giving thought to our marriages, leads us to slowly drift apart.

Marriage is not like the natural, seemingly accidental beauty of the Grand Canyon; it's far more like the completion of a great cathedral that has slowly taken shape over decades. When couples say "I do" on their wedding days, I wish they'd add "and I will, every day of our lives."

Choose to remind yourselves of those blessed words spoken on your wedding day, "I do," and then add the phrase "and I will."

Many waters cannot quench love; rivers cannot sweep it away.
—Song of Songs 8:7

Reflect on your vows. Have you truly been faithful to them? How can you be even more faithful to them now and in the future?

Be Honest, Be Intimate

Intimate acceptance between spouses requires one of the things we all fear most: honesty.

If we want to pursue a true oneness, we have got to stop with the secrets. We lose the satisfaction of being fully known and loved when we hide from our spouses because we begin to think, "Sure, she respects me now, but that's only because she doesn't know about x, y, or z."

Every lie becomes a wedge between the two of you, and here's what's so alarming: the pressures of life will continue to widen that wedge. It is impossible to be an intimate mate with your spouse if you are a total stranger to the truth. Intimacy demands authenticity.

Love does not delight in evil but rejoices with the truth.
—1 Corinthians 13:6

What secrets do you keep from your spouse? Ask God to help you know how to share these with your spouse.

Measure Your Words

Deceit has the potential to push couples apart, but I'm not suggesting we become brutally frank to the point where we hurt our spouses or share things that we know will do more harm than good.

Counselors have told me they hear spouses say things they know the other spouse will never get over. I'm not talking about sharing things like that. What I am saying, however, is that we live "in the light" with each other. We don't hide who we really are.

We need to be completely honest. We also need to measure our words, especially in times of disappointment or anger. Love rejoices in truth, but it is also kind.

Love is kind. —1 Corinthians 13:4

What does your marriage look like ten years from now as you begin living "in the light" today?

Flee Duplicity

Every one of us faces those moments when we know we shouldn't do what we want to do. The fear of being found out can keep us from making the wrong choice, but duplicity undercuts this by saying, "Do what you want, but lie about it."

Duplicity is simply saying, "A second sin can help you enjoy the first sin."

In opposition, honesty says, "You know this is going to break your spouse's heart. You know the consequences will last much longer than the pleasure. You know you can't maintain an intimate marriage and keep this from your spouse, so why do it?" Why get married only to hide?

Adam and his wife were both naked, and they felt no shame.
—Genesis 2:25

What would your marriage look like if you hid nothing? What if you made choices so you had nothing to hide?

Don't Wait

I slid into the restaurant booth first and Lisa snuggled up right next to me, giving a little exclamation of delight. The young woman sitting across from us asked, "Oh, are you cold?"

"No," Lisa said. "He's just been gone all day. I haven't seen him yet."

Be forewarned: the weight of lies increases through the years. After thirty years of marriage, when Lisa snuggled up to me, it made me feel like a king. If I had been lying to her, it would have made me feel like an impostor. And the longer it had been going on, the more frightening it would have been. Her expression of intimacy would have been painful, as I would have thought, "If only she knew…"

"The truth will set you free." —John 8:32

Honesty can be a fearful thing. Write a prayer to God to give any fear you have about honesty to Him.

Truly Become One

Pursing a more intimate union means wrestling with how radical this notion is that two people become one.

This pursuit, though glorious, will go against every selfish fiber in our being. Many people want intimacy in the abstract more than they want it in reality—we want the benefits of being known and loved, but we hate the process of dying to ourselves that it takes to get there.

Some of us get married thinking we really want a life of intimacy, but once the challenges and burdens of intimacy press in on us, we want to go back to being selfish and estranged.

That is why a man leaves his father and mother and is united to his wife, and they become one flesh. —Genesis 2:24

Being honest with yourself, what will true oneness cost you?

Say, "Ours"

Once you get married, everything changes. Nothing is faced alone.

Questions about "mine" and "yours" may be relevant to couples sorting through a divorce, but never to couples who are pursuing marital intimacy. The very notion of "mine" and "yours" means you are living separate lives.

I would never put on one shoe and walk out in the snow, feeling smug that one foot is covered and warm. That would be foolish and borderline mentally disturbed. Yet many "couples" live that way. As long as they, as individuals, get their way, they are astonishingly unconcerned about their other "foot."

In humility value others above yourselves, not looking to your own interests but each of you to the interests of the others.
—PHILIPPIANS 2:3–4

What do you think you need to do to welcome the thought of true marital intimacy in your life?

Be a Blessing

Becoming one requires a fundamental shift in our thinking. We have to think like God did when He blessed Abraham, saying, "I will bless you, and you will be a blessing."

God urges us to be a blessing in the midst of conflict, not just in happy, peaceful harmony. Because God has blessed me, I am called to be a blessing to others.

Thus, there are two questions we can ask within marriage that will take us to two entirely different dimensions—intimacy or estrangement. We can ask, "How can I bless you?" or, "How can I get my needs met?"

"I will bless you…and you will be a blessing." —GENESIS 12:2

First things first, ask God to remind you of the ways He has blessed you. Write down a list.

Give Yourself Completely

Let's quickly review the journey to become one: We have to navigate marriage so that we are sharing in life, not just acting as teammates. We have to be honest with each other. We have to adopt a blessing mentality.

These are all part of the journey toward oneness. The more you become one as a couple, the happier and more satisfied you will be in your marriage. None of this happens by accident. Two people can find themselves falling in love, but nobody "falls" into intimate oneness.

Here's the endgame—my prayer is that the day would come when the two of you can say to each other in the fullest sense of the words, "I am yours."

I am my beloved's and my beloved is mine. —Song of Songs 6:3

How can you give more of yourself—heart and soul—to your spouse?

Stay Thankful

What if your spouse wants nothing to do with becoming one? This is a painful situation with limited options. But there are some things you can do:

First, get your needs met through appropriate channels. It's not ideal, but if your spouse is unresponsive relationally, cultivate stronger same-gender friendships.

Second, remember someone who has it worse. This helps stir our hearts with thankfulness for the blessings we do have, even if they're small.

Third, focus on the strengths your marriage has. Talk about them, build on them, and thank God for them.

Finally, brothers and sisters…if anything is excellent or praiseworthy —think about such things. —Philippians 4:8

Look for every little thing your spouse does well today and write them down. Thank God for each thing.

Remember You Have God

If you're married to an unusually selfish person, a controlling person, a depressed person, or even if you're wed to just an average sinner, on some days you may say to yourself, "Today, I just need a short break."

You're not taking a break from your marriage, of course, but you are taking a break from working on your marriage. Take whatever good is offered, and just let everything else go.

I've noticed people who are always trying to make their marriages better rarely feel satisfied. They focus so much on what is wrong that they can never enjoy what's right. Remember, no matter how much is wrong, at least one very important thing is right: You have God.

*Blessed is the people whose God is the L*ORD. —P*SALM* 144:15

Write, "Today, I'm taking a break," and rest today in the truth that you have God.

Let God Help

When marriage gets hard for too long, it's easy to want to quit. If you feel this way, God promises two things you need.

First, He promises to renew your will. Just because we feel "done" with our marriage doesn't mean God is. He promises to strengthen our resolve for our marriages.

Second, He enables us to work. We all know there's plenty of work to do in making marriage thrive. When we trust in God, He becomes a powerful divine force lifting us above our apathy and limitations.

It is God who works in you to will and to act in order to fulfill his good purpose. —Philippians 2:13

Whether you feel like quitting or not, write a letter of surrender to God, asking for His help.

Come to Your End

I will applaud anyone who wants to build a good marriage, but too many people try to do it on their own. These people need to come to the end of themselves.

They need to realize that a good marriage as God designed it requires three people, not two.

Only God is enough. Only as two spouses pursue God together will they find the happiness and fulfilment in marriage they long for. God doesn't present Himself as either a "visitor" or an "accessory" to marriage, but as the foundation and loving force that builds it and holds it together.

"Come to me, all you who are weary and burdened, and I will give you rest." —Matthew 11:28

How can the two of you build your marriage by pursuing God— individually and together—more purposefully?

Pray!

The first step to turning around a marriage on the brink of divorce is prayer. It also happens to be the most important step for any couple at any stage of marriage.

I'll admit, prayer is a mystery. But Noah prayed. So did Abraham, Isaac, and Jacob. Moses also prayed, and Joshua, David, Solomon, and all the Old Testament prophets. Even Jesus prayed, and remarkably, the only thing the disciples asked Jesus to teach them was how to pray.

Pray alone. Pray together. Pray all the time. Seek the Lord's will daily for yourself individually, as a couple, and as parents. It will move your marriage into places you've never yet discovered.

"Lord, teach us to pray." —Luke 11:1

Prayer is just like conversation. Practice by writing out a prayer to God.

Fix Right, Build Right

Marriage isn't easy, but at least it's simple to understand what builds a good one.

Always start with prayer. Union with God always strengthens union with a spouse. Then communicate, and learn how to do it well. Not overreacting, truly listening, laughing at misunderstandings, and expressing forgiveness are essential.

Stay connected to godly counselors. Isolation is a big step toward a painful marriage. Also stay connected to each other by finding a common pursuit. Devotionals for couples can be great for this.

Lastly, recognize that trials can make your weaknesses stronger as God uses them to make you more like Him.

The LORD watches over the way of the righteous. —PSALM 1:6

Describe how you would like these five areas to look in your life one year from now.

Love Deeply

There were those on my high school track team who just hated doing intervals. Intervals are intense workouts designed to make you faster.

I liked doing intervals, even though they hurt, because I understood one thing: Every foot race is about going fast. In the end, it's not form, uniform, or appearance that matters, but only speed.

Christian ethics have a similar "this is all that really matters" element—love. We like to focus on individual points of piety— dating/courting, smoking, drinking, gambling, gossip, etc. But the one question God asks us is, "Have you learned to love?"

Now that…you have sincere love for each other, love one another deeply, from the heart. —1 PETER 1:22

How are you doing when it comes to love? Do you love deeply?

Don't Be a Spider

I hate the concept of spider webs—the product of an insect that literally seeks to trap passersby, pulling them into its own world in order to consume them.

Some spouses are like that. They construct marital webs by attracting spouses they think will meet their needs—for approval, sex, support, or finances.

It's easy to slip into being a spider spouse, and even to make it sound right by couching it in romantic language. For a Christian, however, our highest desire for our spouse is not what we can get from them, but how we can love, serve, and support them.

Walk in the way of love, just as Christ loved us and gave himself up for us. —Ephesians 5:2

Ask God to help you identify any areas of your marriage where you've become a spider spouse. What can you do to love better?

Answer This Question

On my wedding day, God and I were trying to achieve two entirely different aims. I wanted to be loved. God wanted me to learn how to love.

I didn't realize this until God cornered me with this question, "Why did you get married?" I had to answer honestly—the way she looked, acted, thought, and my view of her as a potential parent—these were all things I wanted, selfishly so.

No one has challenged me when I suggest that virtually all of us get married for selfish reasons. But we have to get over that if we want to move into a sacred marriage.

Dear children, let us not love with words or speech but with actions and in truth. —1 JOHN 3:18

Why did you get married?

Learn to Love

Most of us are eager to get married because we want to find someone who will always be 100 percent faithful, be there whenever we need them to be, never falter in their love, forgive us when we falter in ours, and who will stay with us until the very end.

Pause for just a moment. Who does that sound like, really?

No person will ever be able to live up to that need, but God has already met it and continues to every day. God and God alone loves us with unfailing love. Our greatest need, then, is to receive His love and learn to love the same way.

We love because he first loved us. —1 JOHN 4:19

Consider God's love that you have received. Truly meditate on it and let it sink deep. Write down your thoughts.

Define True Love

What causes you to love your spouse? Is it her grace, his kindness, her strength, his humor, or anything else you see in them?

I won't say it's bad to appreciate these things about our spouses, but I do have to make one thing clear: All of these are inferior reasons and inferior loves. If I love my spouse because she is kind, I actually love kindness, not my spouse. If I love my spouse because she is thoughtful, it's actually thoughtfulness that I love.

True love is found in absolute benevolence—taking action for someone's highest good regardless of the person's actions or character. This is the love God has shown for us.

This is how we know what love is: Jesus Christ laid down his life for us.
—1 JOHN 3:16

Write a prayer to God confessing how you need His help to love your spouse with true love.

Tap the Source

Absolute benevolence is another way of describing lifelong love. If I love my spouse just because I love her, I don't love her because she's healthy, young, beautiful, wealthy, or godly, so I won't stop loving her if those qualities change.

Since marriage calls us to absolute benevolence, it requires nothing less than the presence of God—the only true source of such love.

Absolute benevolence is born not by trying harder, but by receiving God's love and passing it on. This might sound overly spiritual, but it's the most practical advice I can give you. We just can't love this way on our own.

God is love. Whoever lives in love lives in God, and God in them.
—1 JOHN 4:16

Rest from thinking about your spouse today. How are you doing at loving God?

Love Tough

Absolute benevolence does not mean you let your spouse run over you. I received an email from a wife whose husband said that part of accepting him was accepting that he was an alcoholic and was going to get drunk. Love does not stand by while another person ruins himself.

This means that to find the right way to act, I simply ask, from God's perspective, what is truly best for my spouse? That tells me what I will do.

This expression of absolute benevolence—true love—can be harder than enabling our spouses' dysfunctions. But remember that God's love does not enable our sins; instead, it disciplines us to become like Him.

God disciplines us for our good, in order that we may share in his holiness. —Hebrews 12:10

What changes do you need to make to pursue what is truly best for your spouse?

Get Over Infatuation.

I have nothing against feeling "in love," but feeling in love is not lifelong love.

Feeling in love is just that: a feeling. Feelings change. They are fickle. What I've seen in most couples is when that feeling of being in love dims or goes away completely, panic and doubt begin to set in.

There's no need to overreact when feelings change. They're going to change! That feeling will go away at some point in marriage, and it will probably come back, but whether it goes or comes again isn't the point. The point is choosing biblical love—lifelong love—whether we feel like it or not.

Love never fails. —1 CORINTHIANS 13:8

How are you doing with being "in love?" Now, how are you doing with choosing biblical love?

Examine Your Love

I often hear something like this: "Look, I do all the housework, I get the kids where they need to go, I put them to bed, I work a part-time job on top of all of that, and all he does is sit on his rear end as soon as he gets home from his eight-hour-a-day job."

1 Corinthians 13 describes how love behaves. According to God's description of love, a statement like the one above falls short of God's love, because love doesn't boast. To God, attitudes matter as much as actions.

Yes, I would have words for the husband in this case, too, but we mustn't allow our spouse's failure to love assault our decision to love. Each of us will be challenged by love in different ways.

Love is patient, love is kind. It does not envy, it does not boast, it is not proud. —1 CORINTHIANS 13:4

Read 1 Corinthians 13. How can you intentionally love your spouse like that this week?

Step Up

The sixty-something-year-old woman kept wiping away the tears until she could tell her story.

"I've worked at a hospice for twenty years. Caring for people is what I do. Yet I resented doing the very things for my husband that I spent my whole day doing for others." She paused, and then said, "Until, that is, my husband got cancer. I started caring for him. It was the best season of marriage we've ever had."

Most people think their marriages will improve when their spouses step up. This wife said her marriage improved when she stepped up.

Now that you know these things, you will be blessed if you do them.
—JOHN 13:17

Are you serving others more than you serve your spouse? Explain.

Separate Love from Desire

One of the greatest misconceptions today among both singles and couples is in our understanding of the words "desire" and "love." The two are not the same, but we think they are.

A five-year-old "loves" candy in the sense that he desires it. In the same way, an immature twenty-five-year-old says he "loves" a woman because he desires her. When the five-year-old eats the candy, it is destroyed. When the twenty-five-year-old sleeps with a woman he desires but is not married to, he dishonors her. Both cases are examples of consuming, not loving.

The words and concepts are not synonyms, though of course they can coexist. As long as we mix up the two, however, we will misunderstand both, and we will never understand what constitutes a truly sacred marriage.

Greater love has no one than this: to lay down one's life for one's friends.
—John 15:13

Are you consuming your spouse, or are you loving him or her? Explain.

Choose to Love

When we separate love from desire, we see how silly it is when a married woman says, "I love him, but I'm just not in love with him anymore."

The more loving I act toward someone, the more I desire them. A wayward parent who ignores his kids is capable of astonishing apathy, but parents who love their kids in a practical way can't stop caring. Your acts of love soften your heart, just as acts of apathy harden it.

In marriage, however, we have this crazy notion that desire must come first—I want to be with you. Most of the world thinks a marriage is over when we stop desiring. God says our marriages suffer when we stop loving. That's a huge difference.

Love must be sincere. —Romans 12:9

How are you doing at letting love create desire, instead of letting lack of desire lead to a lack of love?

Revel in God's Love

Since there is such a difference between desire and love, the goal of our marriages must change.

Many spouses don't realize what they are asking is, "How can I still desire a man who is so selfish?" "How can I still desire a woman who criticizes everything I do?" The root of these questions is the assumption that desire is the all-important commodity for a happy, fulfilling marriage.

But that's not the biblical goal. The biblical goal is a shared experience of God living in us and God's love being made complete in us. I may not desire a wife who doesn't respect me, but I can revel in the love God pours out on me and, out of that abundance, pour it out on others.

If we love one another, God lives in us and his love is made complete in us. —1 JOHN 4:12

Describe biblical love in your own words.

Build Desire

"Gary," the young wife explained to me, "I want to have a rocking sex life with my husband, but he criticizes everything I do. I just can't bear to have another aspect of marriage where I'm messing up."

Achieving sexual satisfaction will all but force you to develop the same relational skills that serve all aspects of marriage: humility, the ability to hear hard words and put someone else's needs first, and to be as naked in conversation as you are in each other's arms.

Sex is an easy measuring stick. Problems in other areas of marriage steal desire from the bedroom, but real love expressed throughout marriage will create desire in the bedroom.

You have stolen my heart with one glance of your eyes.
—SONG OF SONGS 4:9

How is your sex life? How can you express love outside the bedroom to build desire within the bedroom?

Take the Time

Frankly, I'm of the opinion that God likely wishes we'd have far more sex, not less. But building the sex life we want takes time.

I was once seated at a table with six Christian sexual therapists. They believed that marital sex takes twenty years to reach its peak, at which point it can be more enjoyable than ever.

This isn't built with gimmicks or tricks, but by love throughout the marriage. Love and love alone will build the trust and vulnerability that make sex amazing for both husbands and wives. Love sustains desire; desire doesn't sustain love.

May you rejoice in the wife of your youth....may you ever be intoxicated with her love. —Proverbs 5:18–19

Plan a conversation with your spouse to talk about building love and desire over time. What will you say?

Live to Give

Have you ever asked yourself what your sin is costing you? When we cultivate any sin that consumes our time, something else has to die, and it's usually the good things that do.

Instead of focusing simply on not doing that sin, why not use temptation as a reminder to perform an act of love? Do someone's chore. Write a letter of encouragement. Pick out an unexpected present. Send an email or text to someone you love.

We can actually use temptation to become more like Christ. This might sound crazy, but not if we understand that for the Christian, to live is to give.

"My command is this: Love each other as I have loved you."
—JOHN 15:12

Plan ahead. What will you do the next time temptation to sin comes?

Peel Off Selfishness

Think of selfishness like wet, dirty clothes. It's miserable taking them off—pulling the wet shirt over your head, sliding the pants down, trying not to get dirt everywhere. But think how wonderful it feels when you get those clothes off, take a shower, and put on something fresh!

We've got to peel off our selfishness. Jesus Himself promised it is better to give than to receive.

Why complain that you do all the giving and rarely receive? According to Jesus, you have a spectacular arrangement! You are laying aside huge heavenly rewards, and your poor spouse is just sitting in those cold, damp, filthy clothes. You should feel sorry for him or her, not for yourself!

"It is more blessed to give than to receive." —Acts 20:35

Write as many benefits to being a giver as you can think of. Then ask God to give you more.

Remain In Love

Intimate marriage isn't built on the big moments. Those can be fun times, but the divorce court is littered with marriages that enjoyed occasional parties amid a wasteland of otherwise persistent apathy.

When you notice a malaise seeping into your marriage, it's tempting to think you can fix things with one big act of repentance. The problem is you can't keep a grand gesture going.

To truly grow our love, it's better to start small and be consistent rather than try to rescue things with a grand gesture.

"As the Father has loved me, so have I loved you. Now remain in my love." —John 15:9

Name three small acts of love you can do for your spouse over the course of the next ten days.

Leave No Regrets

When I think of "lifelong love," I think of Jim and Anne Pierson, who had that blessed single identity.

Sadly, Jim had a long and difficult death from cancer. I fought back tears with Anne as we remembered her wonderful husband, and she told me, "I've had such a good life, Gary; such a good, good life, investing in others and sharing that with Jim."

God wants this for you. He wants you to say good-bye to your lifelong love with similar words. You just have to be what Jim and Anne were: worshipers of God, intent on seeking first His kingdom and righteousness, investing in the lives of others, and reaping eternal rewards.

"They will be like a well-watered garden…and my people will be filled with my bounty." —JEREMIAH 31:12–,14

What legacy do you want your marriage to leave behind?